Bar

In Col

Series Editor: Philip Lamb

Presbus
PUBLISHING

INTRODUCTION

Barton in Colour

First published 2012

ISBN 978 0 9565061 5 3

© **Presbus Publishing** 2012

Published by Presbus Publishing,
Unit 19, Portsmouth Enterprise Centre,
Quartremaine Road, Portsmouth PO3 5QT
Tel: 02392 655224
E-mail: presbusps@aol.com

Design and layout: Robert Wilcockson

Printed by Broadway Creative Printing Services Ltd,
Portsmouth PO3 5QT

Previous page: **The mid-1960s witnessed a London invasion as significant numbers of '7RTs' (Leyland PD2/1s) joined the Barton fleet. Pictured inside Ilkeston garage are Nos 1033 (OLD 646), 1110 (MXX 34) and 1036 (OLD 575), formerly London Transport RTL1537, RTL1335 and RTL1479 respectively.** *PRESBUS ARCHIVE*

This, the fifth volume in the 'Return Journey' series, looks at Barton Transport, one of the country's largest and best-loved independent operators. It does not, however, set out to provide comprehensive coverage of Barton's routes, locations served etc and is certainly not intended to trace the history of the company or its fleet; rather it is a photographic collection illustrating some of the huge variety of vehicles, both new and second-hand, that passed through Barton's hands during what can best be described as the closing years of its postwar heyday. Indeed, it was only in the 1970s that this variety began to diminish — a consequence of the large influx of coaches built to bus-grant specification and thereby qualifying for Government subsidy; yet, given Barton's long-standing propensity for using coaches on stage-carriage services, its predilection for the 'grant coach' was perhaps inevitable.

Even in its final decade Barton continued to command interest and respect, both from enthusiasts and from within the industry itself. It was indeed a sad day in 1989 when the operator, which had run its first bus service in 1908, was effectively merged with local rival Trent. Vehicles, in a simplified livery, continued to display Barton fleetnames, but, with former Trent vehicles drafted in, the magic was fast ebbing away. Today the combined operation continues to trade as Trent Barton, but with the widespread introduction of dedicated liveries for individual routes the identities of the constituent companies have been largely diluted.

Among the locations featured in this book are Nottingham's old bus stations. Looking back at these in 2012 brings a stark reminder that it is not merely the buses that have changed but also the circumstances in which they operate; today our concept of bus travel is completely different from what it was half a century ago. There are other iconic locations too, notably the former bus station at Melton Mowbray (still a coach park), where the imposing façade of the town's library has provided the backdrop for numerous bus pictures; also the old St Margaret's bus station in Leicester, since completely remodelled. Both are well represented here, as indeed are those Barton garage frontages with their red doors and bold signs proclaiming their ownership, now gone but not forgotten.

Most of the photographs that follow date from between 1965 and 1975 — an era when colour film was expensive, many of the then established bus photographers preferring to persevere with black-and-white. Good results were attainable in colour but really only on transparency film, and with slow film speeds added into the equation (not to mention the limitations of affordable SLR cameras), those behind the lens were mindful of wasting film and so tended to restrict their efforts to static vehicles in bus stations or depot yards. These were the cameraman's hunting grounds, where, given good light, he could snap a number of buses at a relatively low shutter speed, thereby ensuring that when his slides were returned to him from the processor there was little or no wastage.

In conclusion I should like thank those who have made pictures available for inclusion, notably Malcolm Keeley, of The Transport Museum, Wythall, and Trevor Follows, custodian of the work of one of the great unsung heroes of bus photography, the late Derek Bailey. Finally, I must confess to not knowing the origin of some of the photographs which, over the years, have joined the Presbus Publishing archive; if your work appears here uncredited, please let me know.

PHILIP LAMB
Portsmouth
June 2012

Above: **A remarkable assortment of Barton hardware on display at Nottingham's Huntingdon Street bus station includes, from the left, Weymann Fanfare-bodied AEC Reliance No 927 (SNN 399), Duple Yeoman-bodied Ford 510E No 815 (815 CNN), Duple Super Vega-bodied Bedford SB1 No 821** (821 CVO) and, partially obscured, Yeates Fiesta FE44-bodied Bedford SB5 No 1026 (508 GUY). Completing the scene are a pair of Trent Leyland PD2s and one of Barton's Willowbrook-bodied Leyland PS1 rebuilds.
T. C. BASSINDALE / THE TRANSPORT MUSEUM, WYTHALL

3

Left: **Seen in at Huntingdon Street on 4 August 1962 is 554 (KAL 151), a Leyland Tiger PS1 with Duple 'A' coachwork, new in 1948. Many of these fine coaches would later be rebuilt as double-deckers.** DEREK BAILEY

Below: **Some three years previously, on 1 March 1959, Huntingdon Street was playing host to No 631 (LNN 802), a Beccols-bodied Barton BTS1/1 constructed in 1950 using parts from a prewar Leyland Lion.** DEREK BAILEY

Left: **In the 1960s Nottingham boasted no fewer that three bus stations, all of which were served by Barton. Seen waiting to depart Huntingdon Street for Calverton is No 516 (JVO 233), one of a number of forward-entrance, lowbridge Duple-bodied Leyland PD1s placed in service in 1947/8. These elegant, well-appointed vehicles had straight staircases which rose across the bus behind the driver's cab — a feature destined to appear on further Barton double-deckers in the years to come.** PRESBUS ARCHIVE

Left: **On 1 June 1967 No 722 (RAL 37),** another BTS1/1 but with Plaxton Venturer II coachwork, loads in Leicester's St Margaret's bus station. Following Barton's takeover of Robin Hood Coaches, in 1961, vehicles carried the Robin Hood motif as well as the familiar Barton pennant. *DEREK BAILEY*

Right: **Another of Nottingham's bus stations** was situated in Mount Street, and adjacent to the bus station itself was Barton's parking ground, where vehicles of many types could be found on layover. Pictured resting between duties on 3 June 1972 is No 743 (SVO 44), a Plaxton Venturer II-bodied AEC Reliance, one of nine dating from 1954. Behind is Duple-bodied Leyland PD1 No 471 (JNN 464), by now some 25 years old but still looking very serviceable, as indeed does the 18-year-old Reliance. *DEREK BAILEY*

Right: **Back in Huntingdon Street bus** station we find all-Leyland PD2/12 No 731 (RAL 333) awaiting departure on route 7A (Nottingham–Calverton). A highbridge bus, one of a pair new in 1952 with conventional open rear platform, it was modified by the addition of platform doors in 1959. *PRESBUS ARCHIVE*

Left: **Pictured on a Nottingham local service, No 735 (VVO 735) was a Leyland PSI/I renumbered and re-registered in 1957 upon receipt of this attractive lowbridge Willowbrook body, the chassis having previously formed the basis of Duple-bodied coach No 560 (KAL 380). Many Barton double-deckers carried between-decks advertising for Barton's coastal services.** HILLSIDE PUBLISHING

Right: **The yards at Barton's headquarters at Chilwell provided a constant source of interest. Parked up on 3 August 1968 were a pair of unusual AEC Reliance coaches dating from 1954. No 750 (RTA 228), with rare Strachans coachwork, had been new to Wakley of Axminster, joining the Barton fleet when just a year old, while No 778 (MHO 362), with, if anything, even rarer Mann Egerton coachwork, was acquired from Talbott, Moreton-in-Marsh, in 1958.** DEREK BAILEY

Left: **Barton's Leyland rebuilds were regular performers on service 7A. Here No 788 (XVO 788), a Tiger PSI rebuilt in 1957 and fitted with well-proportioned lowbridge bodywork by Northern Counties, awaits departure from Huntingdon Street on 27 May 1972.** MALCOLM KEELEY

Right: **Another view of the rare Mann Egerton-bodied AEC Reliance. Acquired by Barton from Talbott, Moreton-in-Marsh, No 778 (MHO 362) had been new in 1954 to Creamline, of Bordon, Hants. It is seen here parked in the depot yard at Long Eaton, awaiting its next tour of duty.** *PRESBUS ARCHIVE*

Below right: **Our first visit to Nottingham's Broad Marsh bus station finds No 795 (795 BAL) about to depart for Ruddington on 4 April 1970. This was yet another Leyland PS1/1 rebuilt by Barton, in this instance in 1958, the chassis having previously formed the basis of coach No 550 (KAL 147). Despite being of lowbridge configuration, the replacement Northern Counties body has more that a hint of a Southdown 'Queen Mary' about it ...** *DEREK BAILEY*

Far right: **From the same batch of rebuilds was No 799 (799 BAL), which utilised the Leyland PS1 chassis of coach No 561 (KAL 381) but for some reason was blessed with an AEC Regent V-style grille, which gave the bus an altogether different aspect. It was photographed at Chilwell on 8 June 1969.** *DEREK BAILEY*

Above: **AEC Reliance 801 (RHO 905)** was new in 1955 to Creamline of Bordon, its Duple Britannia body style having been introduced earlier that year to replace the short-lived Elizabethan. Acquired by Barton in 1958, the coach is seen departing Leicester for Nottingham.
PRESBUS ARCHIVE

Right: Also acquired by Barton in 1958, No 804 (PDD 980) was another AEC Reliance, this time with late-model Duple Elizabethan bodywork. New in 1955 to Marchant of Cheltenham, it was photographed in Nottingham's Huntingdon Street bus station.
T. C. BASSINDALE / THE TRANSPORT MUSEUM, WYTHALL

Far right: **AEC Bridgemaster 805 (76 MME)** was a former demonstrator, purchased in 1958 when just a year old, having previously been demonstrated in Barton livery. It is seen here at Chilwell on 30 April 1967. Similar demonstrators found their way into the Birmingham City Transport and South Wales Transport fleets.
DEREK BAILEY

Far left: **A number of Alexander-bodied Leyland Tiger Cubs and AEC Reliances were purchased in the period 1954-60. These proved to be excellent workhorses and were regarded as dual-purpose vehicles, perpetuating Barton's policy of using coaches rather than saloon buses on routes requiring single-deckers. One of six Reliances new in 1959, No 811 (811 CAL) was caught parked up in Nottingham awaiting its next duty on route 14 to Beeston Rylands, a large residential area to the south of the city centre.** *PRESBUS ARCHIVE*

Left: **A visit to Chilwell as part of an enthusiasts' tour on 27 May 1972 revealed this gem. Metro-Cammell-bodied Leyland PD1 No 819 (HF 9598) had been new to Wallasey Corporation in 1946 but was acquired by Barton from Phillips of Holywell, in 1959. By the time of the photograph it had become a service vehicle — minus its roof, Morecambe-style, for tree-lopping duties, yet still, it would seem, upholding the Barton tradition of carrying parcels!** *MALCOLM KEELEY*

Left: **A lot of coaches were delicensed during the winter months, spending many a cold night in the yard at Chilwell. Seen here displaying a 'NOT LICENSED' board is No 829 (829 ENN), a solitary Burlingham Seagull 60-bodied Bedford SB1 new in 1959.** *PRESBUS ARCHIVE*

Left: **In 1959 Barton acquired no fewer than 14 all-Leyland PD1s from Leicester City Transport, the buses dating from 1946. Pictured at Ilkeston on 8 August 1969 with a pair of Duple-bodied PD1s for company is No 844 (DJF 339), formerly LCT No 238.** *DEREK BAILEY*

Right: **Seen parked up on the forecourt at Melton Mowbray in 13 August 1967 is lowbridge all-Leyland PD1 No 855 (JDE 7), new in 1947 to Green's of Haverfordwest. Having passed with that concern to Western Welsh, it had been acquired by Barton in 1960 and seven years later certainly looked its age when compared with No 1088 (MXX 78), formerly London Transport RTL1355. Peering out from within the garage is Plaxton Panorama-bodied AEC Reliance No 864 (864 HAL).** *DEREK BAILEY*

Left: **The year 1960 also saw the arrival of No 856 (BRN 290), formerly Ribble 'White Lady' No 1230 — an exotic vehicle even by Barton standards. Seen at Huntingdon Street on 10 August 1963, the Burlingham-bodied Leyland PD1/3, a lowbridge 49-seater, would not stay long, being withdrawn and scrapped the following year.** *DEREK BAILEY*

Right: **Plaxton revolutionised the coach industry in 1958 with the introduction of its Panorama body, and, quite naturally, Barton was an early customer, taking delivery of seven on AEC Reliance chassis in 1960.** Pressed into touring service, the last of the batch, No 868 (868 HAL), is seen on a tour of the Lake District. *PRESBUS ARCHIVE*

Below: **Perhaps the best-known Barton bus of all time. New in 1960, No 861 (861 HAL) was an exercise in what was possible rather than what was practical, combining a Dennis Loline III chassis (fitted with a Leyland O.600 engine) with a lowbridge Northern Counties body specially built to an overall height of just 12ft 6in.** Seen on 4 August 1962 departing Nottingham on the 'Derby Express' route 42, the bus was destined to remain unique. *DEREK BAILEY*

Right: **Following its takeover of the Cream Bus Service of Stamford, Barton continued to maintain a presence in the town, some distance from its Chilwell base. Parked up alongside the garage there on 27 February 1971 was No 879 (109 HVO), a rare Yeates Pegasus-bodied Bedford SB1 with set-back front axle. Lurking behind is No 873 (873 HAL), a conventional SB1 with Plaxton Embassy coachwork.** *DEREK BAILEY*

Left: **Looking immaculate in a fresh coat of paint (albeit still awaiting a complete set of fleetnames), No 883 (KGK 731) was one of a pair of ex-London Transport '3RTs' (AEC Regent IIIs) taken over in 1961 with the business of Cream Bus Service. The Cravens-bodied vehicle, pictured in March of that year, was formerly RT1472 and had been acquired by Cream in 1956. It was to serve Barton until 1967.** DEREK BAILEY

Right: **In recent years the old Broad Marsh bus station and its environs have been completely redeveloped, leaving little from which to identify this scene. Long gone too are the lowbridge Barton BTD2 rebuilds using Leyland components from a variety of sources — in the case of No 901 (901 LRR) Yorkshire Woollen. Bodywork, by Northern Counties, was similar to that built on earlier rebuilds of reconditioned PS1 chassis and relied heavily on styling borrowed from Southdown's 'Queen Marys'.** PRESBUS ARCHIVE

Right: **Among the coaches delicensed at Chilwell one winter in the early 1970s we find No 908 (662 KNN), a Duple Super Vega-bodied Bedford SB1, one of three dating from 1961, in which year Barton assumed control of Nottingham-based Robin Hood Coaches. Thereafter the majority of the fleet bore Robin Hood insignia, coaches allocated to former Robin Hood duties displaying (as here) both Barton and Robin Hood fleetnames.** PRESBUS ARCHIVE

Left: **Acquired with the Robin Hood fleet in 1961, No 922 (MAL 739) was a 1950 Leyland Royal Tiger PSU1/15 with Burlingham Seagull coachwork. The coach is seen here on 4 August 1962 at Huntingdon Street.** *DEREK BAILEY*

Left: **Seen about to depart Leicester St Margaret's for Nottingham is Barton 914 (VHO 500), another AEC Reliance/Duple Britannia new to Creamline, Bordon, for Forces' leave work. Creamline renewed its fleet frequently, this 1959-built coach passing to Barton in 1961.** *HILLSIDE PUBLISHING*

Right: **Not to Melbourne, Australia, but to Melbourne, Derbyshire, was the last trip made by this 1960 Duple Vista-bodied Bedford C5Z1 before being laid up at Chilwell. Unique in the Barton fleet, No 935 (149 FVO) was another coach acquired from Robin Hood.** *PRESBUS ARCHIVE*

Right: **In 1962 Barton acquired a trio of all-Leyland PD2/1s from Todmorden JOC. Seen displaying dual fleetnames at Ilkeston on 8 June 1969 is the first of these numerically, No 942 (GWW 41). All three dated from 1947.** *DEREK BAILEY*

Below: **Keeping company with No 942 on the same day was Yeates Europa-bodied AEC Reliance No 946 (946 MRR), also with dual fleetnames. One of a batch of six 36-footers new in 1962, it was an unlikely candidate for stage-carriage work, notwithstanding its original dual-door layout, yet the 15 (Ilkeston–Old Sawley) was a regular haunt. Note the sliding entrance door.** *DEREK BAILEY*

Right: **The acquisition of second-hand Leyland double-deckers, notably with Leyland's own bodywork, continued as the 1960s progressed. Ribble again became the source in 1962, when five lowbridge PD2/3s arrived. Pictured at Chilwell on 30 September 1967 is No 955 (CCK 363).** *DEREK BAILEY*

Left: **Representative of Barton's intake of new double-deckers in the early 1960s, 960 (960 PRR) was a lowbridge Northern Counties-bodied AEC Regent V built to broadly the same configuration as the company's Leyland PD1s of a decade or so previously. It was photographed during the reconstruction of Nottingham's Mount Street bus station in the early-1970s.** *PRESBUS ARCHIVE*

Right: **Barton was an avid supporter of the Bedford VAL, purchasing the type in combination with just about every conceivable make of coachwork. Similar in style to the six AEC Reliances of 1962, Bedford VAL14s Nos 963-9 arrived in 1963 with dual-door Yeates Europa bodies and were used on stage services such as that to Beeston Rylands, as demonstrated here by No 969 (969 RVO) loading in the rebuilt Mount Street bus station.** *PRESBUS ARCHIVE*

Left: **Although attractive in their own right, the Yeates-bodied VALs were no match for this! Photographed when new in May 1963, No 970 (414 SRR), a Plaxton Val-bodied VAL14, represented everything that was great about a British coach in the early 1960s: clean, straight lines, vast areas of glass and just the right amount of brightwork; it was sheer perfection. No 970 and its three sisters were clearly for coaching duties only.** *DEREK BAILEY*

Above: **Even classic coaches were used on work normally associated with saloon buses. One of 10 Harrington Grenadier-bodied AEC Reliance 36-footers received in 1964, No 987 (987 VRR) awaits departure on a Nottingham local service.**
PRESBUS ARCHIVE

Right: **Harrington Legionnaire-bodied Bedford VAL14 No 989 (989 VRR) may have been promoting express services to Weston-super-Mare but was itself less appropriately employed on stage-carriage work at Melton Mowbray on 18 June 1966. Eight such vehicles were taken into stock in 1964.** *DEREK BAILEY*

Left: **On 25 June 1964 newly delivered Duple (Northern)-bodied Bedford SB5 No 998 (998 XNN) prepares to depart Huntingdon Street on the express service to Skegness. The Firefly was a Burlingham design which entered production following the takeover of that concern by Duple, more than 250 being built during its three-season run.** *DEREK BAILEY*

Above: **The last new Bedford VAL14 to join the Barton fleet was a solitary example with Duple Vega Major coachwork. The low build of the VAL is readily apparent in this photograph taken on 22 May 1971 at Chilwell, where No 1000 (ANN 700B) is seen surrounded by other coaches, among them Strachans-bodied AEC Reliance 750 (RTA 228) and Bedford SB5/Harrington Crusader 1025 (BVO 25C).** *DEREK BAILEY*

Right: **For 1965 Harrington supplied no fewer than 25 coaches, of which 10 were Grenadier-bodied AEC Reliances. Among these was No 1008 (BVO 8C), seen at Long Eaton alongside No 1201 (HVO 470K), a Plaxton Panorama Elite II-bodied Bedford YRQ to 'grant coach' specification. The photograph as taken on 14 July 1974.**
MALCOLM KEELEY

Below: **The other 15 coaches for 1965 were Harrington Crusader-bodied Bedford SB5s, which although intended primarily for coaching duties were fitted with full destination screens. Seen following sale in 1973 to Vaggs Coaches of Knockin Heath is the former 1013 (BVO 13C). It would remain in service with Vaggs until 1980, subsequently becoming a mobile shop.**
PRESBUS ARCHIVE

Right: **Barton continued to acquire other operators and their vehicles. From Westward Ho Coach Tours came Burlingham Seagull-bodied Bedford SB EEB 466, which took number 1045 in the Barton fleet. Still in Westward Ho livery but with Barton fleetnames, it was photographed on 18 June 1966.**
DEREK BAILEY

Left: **Not for the first time (or, indeed, the last), the market for second-hand double-deckers was swelled considerably in the mid-1960s by the availability of dozens of former London Transport buses which were by no means past their sell-by dates. LT's '6RTs' (RTWs) and '7RTs' (RTLs) were available to anyone who desired them, and predictably Barton indulged its penchant for second-hand Leylands, purchasing 17 RTLs and a solitary RTW. Seen here between journeys on the 4A Nottingham–Sandiacre service, Barton 1046 (OLD 597) had previously been RTL1488.** *PRESBUS ARCHIVE*

Below: **Seen at St Margaret's, Leicester, on 8 July 1968, Barton 1058 (45 DJF) had been acquired in 1966 with the city's old-established Provincial business. Dating from 1962, it was a fine example of the 36ft AEC Reliance fitted with Plaxton Panorama coachwork.** *DEREK BAILEY*

Right: **The end of the Barton double-deck fleet was fast approaching when this scene was recorded at Ilkeston Market on 27 May 1972. Following the influx of ex-London Transport types and a quartet of Titans from St Helens, the next double-decker to arrive was No 1087 (SAU 199), in 1967. Formerly Nottingham City Transport 199, this was a lowbridge Weymann-bodied AEC Regent III dating from 1954 and was destined to have a short life with Barton.** *MALCOLM KEELEY*

Below: **Following the purchase of former ex-Nottingham AEC Regent III No 1087 Barton acquired a pair of Park Royal-bodied AEC Renowns which had been new to Smith of Barrhead and passed with that firm to Western SMT. Purchased in 1968, they were associated largely with services from Ilkeston, where No 1116 (212 JUS) was photographed on 8 August 1969.** *DEREK BAILEY*

Left: **Looking immaculate as it prepares to depart Leicester St Margaret's at the start of a Scottish tour is No 1091 (LVO 91E), numerically the first of 10 Plaxton Panorama I-bodied AEC Reliances to join the fleet in 1967.** *PRESBUS ARCHIVE*

Above: **Seen at Ilkeston on 8 June 1969 is No 1111 (OLD 796), the one-time RTL1577, from the 1967 intake of former LT rolling stock. Behind is an unidentified Plaxton coach, in all likelihood a Panorama-bodied AEC Reliance.** *DEREK BAILEY*

Left: **In June 1967 Barton acquired the old-established business of Hall Bros of South Shields, which was chiefly engaged in running express services between the North East and the Midlands, hence Barton's interest. At first most Hall Bros coaches ran in Barton livery but with Barton/Hall Bros fleetnames and 'H'-series fleet numbers. This soon faded out, however, the coaches all being renumbered in the main Barton system. Centre-stage in a superb scene that captures perfectly the ambiance of the old bus station at Broad Marsh is No 1121 (BCU 281C), one of two Duple Vega Major-bodied Bedford VAL14s taken into stock as a result of the aforementioned acquisition. Note, however, that by now the coach has been demoted to local-bus work.** *DEREK BAILEY*

Above: **Acquired by Barton from Weardale Motor Services was 1965 AEC Reliance with dual-purpose Willowbrook bodywork, No 1129 (FUP 272C). A similarity of liveries meant that it initially retained the colours of its original owner, being seen thus adorned shortly after acquisition, in Burleys Way, Leicester, on 7 June 1969.** *DEREK BAILEY*

Left: **Seen at Ilkeston on 21 April 1974, No 1140 (1637 PF) was a rare example of a pure service bus in the Barton fleet. A Willowbrook-bodied AEC Reliance, it had been new to Safeguard, Guildford, in 1963 and came to Barton in 1969. Representing the new order alongside is 'grant coach' 1199 (HVO 468K), a Plaxton Panorama Elite II-bodied Bedford YRQ.** *DEREK BAILEY*

Left: **Barton's** decision to standardise on 'grant coaches' (suitable for stage-carriage work and thus qualifying for a Government grant) had a wide-reaching effect; besides spelling the end of the double-decker it heralded the gradual run-down of the varied coach fleet purchased prior to 1970. The first true grant coaches were 10 AEC Reliances with Plaxton Panorama Elite Express bodywork delivered in 1970, of which No 1148 (DAL 773J) is seen loading for Nottingham in Melton Mowbray bus station on 1 November 1974.
DEREK BAILEY

Right: **A Duple Viscount-bodied Ford R192 dating from 1966, No 1154 (CFT 203D)** was acquired by Barton with the business of Taylor Bros of North Shields. It was photographed at Stamford, wearing full Barton livery, but with Hall Bros fleetnames. Taylor Bros vehicles were assigned to Hall Bros following acquisition.
PRESBUS ARCHIVE

Right: **Also from Taylor Bros came No 1157 (GFT 964), a 1963 Duple Bella Vega-bodied Bedford SB8.** It was photographed on 23 July 1972 on an excursion to Skegness.
DEREK BAILEY

Above: **Running as a duplicate on the X81 Coventry–Newcastle service, ex-Taylor Bros Plaxton Embassy III-bodied Bedford SB5 No 1163 (JFT 258) was caught at Leeming Services on the A1 on 9 April 1971.** *DEREK BAILEY*

Right: **Seen in earlier guise, with branding for the Tyneside–Midlands Express and Hall Bros fleetnames and fleet number, is No 1169 (ACU 306C), a 1965 Harrington Grenadier-bodied Leyland Leopard PSU3/3R.** *PRESBUS ARCHIVE*

Right: **Unusually, Barton in 1971 purchased bespoke dual-purpose saloons in the shape of 11 Willowbrook-bodied Bedford YRQ 45-seaters, Nos 1179-89. Pictured at Chilwell on 3 June 1972 is No 1181 (GAL 14J).** *DEREK BAILEY*

Above: **Delivery of grant coaches really got underway in 1971/2 with a mix of Bedford YRQs and Leyland Leopards. Seen in Durham on a private-hire duty in October 1974 is No 1205 (LAL 307K), numerically the first of a batch of 15 Plaxton Panorama Elite II Express-bodied Leopard PSU3B/4Rs.** *PRESBUS ARCHIVE*

Right: **Although the majority were bodied by Plaxton, many grant coaches received Duple Dominant coachwork, among them No 1315 (WRR 353M), one of 36 Bedford YRTs delivered in 1973 and which swept away many of the older types that had for so long typified the Barton fleet. Note the two-piece power-operated doors — an essential provision under the grant scheme. The location is Melton Mowbray, the date 18 July 1976.** *DEREK BAILEY*

Right: **The business of Lees Motorways, Nottingham, was acquired in 1974. Seen in the yard at Chilwell on 21 April is a selection of the rolling stock that passed to Barton as part of the deal, all displaying Barton fleet numbers and 'Barton Transport' stickers. Centre-stage is No 1447 (589 EYU), a Duple Continental-bodied AEC Reliance that had been new to Global, London, in 1963. It later received full Barton livery. Also visible are a pair of Plaxton Panorama I-bodied AEC Reliances.** *DEREK BAILEY*

Below: **Following the delivery of No 1464, 1000 was dropped from the fleet-numbering sequence. Seen in Gravel Street, Leicester, on 3 July 1982 is 476 (MNU 476P), a Plaxton Supreme Express-bodied Leyland Leopard PSU3C/4R, which was sporting a Supreme IV dash panel in addition to an experimental livery. It seems that Barton, like everyone else, was trying to keep up with the times, but it need not have bothered — the traditional Barton livery simply could not be improved!** *TREVOR FOLLOWS*

Left: **Another non-standard livery was applied to No 541 (FTO 541V), a Plaxton Supreme IV-bodied Leyland Leopard PSU3E/4R, seen at East Midlands Airport in June 1984. The 737 was a fast link between the airport and Nottingham city centre.** *TREVOR FOLLOWS*

Below: **Following the Leyland/Bedford era Barton formed a new allegiance and, aside from five Leyland Tigers delivered in 1983, standardised on DAF chassis, a total of 31 — all with Plaxton Paramount coachwork — being taken into stock before the company sold out to Trent in 1989. Pictured at Melton Mowbray in May 1987 is DAF MB200/ Paramount 3200 No 623 (B623 JRC), new in 1985.** *TREVOR FOLLOWS*

Above: **And finally … The date is 1 June 1987, and Barton 635 (D635 WNU), a Plaxton Paramount 3200-bodied DAF MB230** new the previous year, takes a break at Fort William while on an extended tour. As well turned out as ever and in the best tradition of Barton's coaches, it looks … well, perfect! *MALCOLM KEELEY*